THE POCKET AGILE BIBLE

Shorter Than Your Sprint, Smarter Than Your Last Standup

Riccardo Barbieri

Copyright © 2024 by Riccardo Barbieri.

All rights reserved. No part of this book may be reproduced, stored in a retrieval system, or transmitted in any form or by any means, electronic, mechanical, photocopying, recording, or otherwise, without prior written permission from the publisher, except for brief quotations embodied in critical reviews and certain other noncommercial uses permitted by copyright law.

TABLE OF CONTENTS

Introduction 7
Chapter 1 - Introduction to Agile: More Than a Buzzword 16
Chapter 2 - Understanding Agile Frameworks 26
Chapter 3 - The Agile Mindset 38
Chapter 5 - Roles in Agile Teams 60
Chapter 6 - Core Practices for Agile Excellence 72
Chapter 7 - Quality Control and Continuous Improvement 84
Chapter 8 - Starting the Agile Journey 98
Chapter 9 - Scaling Agile Across the Organization 111
Chapter 10 - Case Studies and Lessons Learned 124
Chapter 11 - Essential Agile Tools and Techniques 138
Chapter 12 - Templates for Agile Teams 153
Chapter 13 - Resources for Continuous Learning 165

Introduction

Welcome to The Pocket Agile Bible—a guide to mastering Agile excellence, shaping high-performing teams, and embracing a mindset that empowers you to achieve remarkable results in today's fast-paced world of product development and organizational change. This book is more than just a set of instructions for how to implement Scrum, Kanban, or Lean principles. It's about transforming the way you think, the way you approach challenges, and most importantly, how you lead yourself and your teams toward success.

Let me share a bit about myself and why I'm so passionate about Agile. I've spent over a decade building software products and leading teams in diverse industries, from e-commerce to publishing, banking, and the luxury watch industry. My journey has been shaped by a series of experiences that started in the traditional world of waterfall development, and over time, took me into the transformative world of Agile.

I began my career working in environments where change was slow, requirements were set in stone, and project plans were sacred. It wasn't long before I realized that this way of working often led to missed opportunities, frustrated teams, and products that didn't quite hit the mark. I knew there had to be a better way, a way to move faster, collaborate better, and deliver products that people truly wanted. That's when I found Agile—and my career was never the same.

What I didn't know at the time was that the Agile methodologies I had heard so much about—Scrum, Kanban, Lean—would completely transform not just the way I worked, but also how I viewed leadership, teamwork, and problem-solving. Agile isn't just a framework; it's a mindset. A mindset that fosters continuous improvement, embraces change, and encourages collaboration at every level.

In 2014, I had the opportunity to lead an Agile transformation program at a major organization. This was my baptism by fire—helping a large, established company shift from a rigid waterfall approach to an Agile, flexible, and iterative process. It was difficult at times. There were setbacks, resistance, and even moments of doubt. But ultimately, we succeeded. We broke down silos, fostered trust, and empowered teams to deliver better results, faster. It was in this process that I truly "got" Agile.

From there, my journey continued. I joined the Swatch Group Services in 2019 as a Software Product Owner, where I had the privilege of leading the first Agile development team in the group. This was one of the most exciting experiences of my career—building a high-performing team from scratch and guiding them through the complexities of Agile. It wasn't always easy, but it was incredibly rewarding. It taught me the power of aligning teams with a shared vision, empowering individuals to take ownership, and most importantly, giving them the space to experiment and learn from failure.

Over the years, I've had the chance to work on a variety of products—some of which have revolutionized industries—and across multiple continents, from Bologna to Dubai to Moscow. Each experience has taught me something new about Agile, whether it's understanding how to tailor frameworks to fit different organizational cultures or managing teams that span multiple time zones and geographies. The core principles of Agile remain the same, but the way they're applied can vary greatly depending on the context.

This book is the culmination of my journey—a journey that has shaped my belief that the Agile mindset is not just a set of practices or a methodology but a philosophy that can be applied in all aspects of life. Agile is about breaking free from the constraints of traditional thinking, embracing change, and relentlessly striving for improvement. It's about shifting from a culture of control to one of collaboration, from rigidity to flexibility, from working hard to working smart.

In this guide, I'll walk you through everything

I've learned over the past decade. From the foundations of Agile—what it is, where it came from, and why it's so powerful in modern organizations—to the specific frameworks like Scrum, Kanban, and Lean that can help you turn Agile principles into actionable practices. I'll also dive deep into the Agile mindset—the philosophy that makes Agile not just a set of tools, but a way of being. You'll learn how to apply Agile to your projects, your teams, and your leadership. You'll understand how to foster a culture of continuous improvement, and how to scale Agile across organizations to ensure long-term success.

But let me make one thing clear: this book is not just about theory. It's about practical, real-world application. I've been on the front lines, leading teams through the ups and downs of Agile transformations, and I'm here to share the lessons I've learned—both the successes and the failures. I'll provide you with tools, templates, and resources that you can use right away to start implementing Agile in your own teams and organizations. I've walked this path, and now I want to help you walk it faster, smarter, and more confidently.

As a product manager, I've had to deal with the challenges of balancing competing priorities, managing stakeholder expectations, and ensuring that the teams I lead are aligned with the company's goals. Agile has been the framework that's allowed me to do this effectively. It's given me the tools to manage complexity, uncertainty, and change. It's given me the ability to deliver value incrementally and iteratively, ensuring that we're always focused on what matters most to our customers. But Agile isn't just a framework for product management—it's a philosophy that can be applied across your entire organization. From marketing to operations to customer support, Agile can help you create a culture of collaboration, innovation, and continuous learning.

One of the core beliefs I hold dear is that Agile is for everyone. It's not just for software development teams or product managers. It's for leaders, for marketers, for designers, for HR professionals, for anyone who wants to improve their work, improve their teams, and improve their organizations. The principles of Agile can help you drive change, increase efficiency, and deliver results that matter. Whether you're leading a startup or an enterprise, Agile offers a way to unlock potential and achieve greatness.

I've had the privilege of working in diverse industries, from publishing to banking, e-commerce, and luxury goods. Each industry comes with its own unique challenges, and yet, the principles of Agile have proven to be universally applicable. Whether it's delivering an e-commerce platform that supports millions of customers, or guiding a product development team through the creation of a luxury timepiece, the Agile mindset remains a powerful tool for overcoming obstacles and achieving success.

One of the most exciting aspects of Agile is its adaptability. Agile is not a one-size-fits-all solution. It's a set of guiding principles that you can tailor to fit your organization's needs. It's about taking the time to understand the challenges your team faces, and then using the right Agile tools and frameworks to solve those problems. Over the years, I've worked with Scrum, Kanban, Lean, and hybrid Agile models, and each has its place depending on the situation. My goal in this book is to give you a deep understanding of these frameworks so that you can choose the one that's right for your team and your organization.

But Agile isn't just about processes—it's about people. It's about creating environments where individuals feel safe to experiment, to fail, and to learn. One of the most important lessons I've learned over the years is the importance of psychological safety. In high-performing Agile teams, people are empowered to speak up, share their ideas, and collaborate without fear of judgment or retribution. This is the foundation for continuous improvement and innovation. As a leader, it's your job to create that environment and ensure that your team has the resources and support they need to succeed.

As you read through The Pocket Agile Bible, I want you to remember one thing: this is your journey. Agile isn't something that happens overnight. It's a continual process of learning, adapting, and improving. But if you commit to it, if you take the time to truly understand and apply Agile principles, you will see remarkable results.

Your teams will become more effective, your products will deliver more value, and your organization will be better equipped to thrive in today's fast-paced, ever-changing world.

Thank you for choosing this book as your guide. It's my hope that the knowledge you gain here will not only help you become an Agile expert but will also inspire you to lead with purpose, drive continuous improvement, and create the kind of teams and organizations that can achieve extraordinary things.

Let's get started. Your journey toward Agile excellence begins now.

Chapter 1 - Introduction to Agile: More Than a Buzzword

What comes to mind when you hear the word "Agile"? Is it flexibility? Speed? Perhaps it's a vision of high-performing teams delivering extraordinary results. Or maybe, it's just another corporate buzzword tossed around in meetings to sound progressive. Whatever your perception, let me tell you this: Agile is not just a methodology; it's a revolution—a transformational approach that reshapes how we work, lead, and deliver value. If you embrace it, Agile can be your secret weapon to unlocking potential, driving innovation, and achieving sustained excellence in any organization.

A Brief History of Agile: How It All Began

To understand the power of Agile, we must first trace its origins. The story of Agile begins not in tech startups or Silicon Valley boardrooms, but on manufacturing floors, in the battlefields of iterative engineering, and even in the halls of creative problem-solving during wartime. The principles that underpin Agile have been evolving for decades.

The roots of Agile can be found in Lean manufacturing, a philosophy pioneered by Toyota in the mid-20th century. Lean principles emphasized minimizing waste, optimizing processes, and delivering value as quickly as possible. These ideas laid the groundwork for iterative thinking and continuous improvement.

Fast forward to the 1990s. The software industry faced a dilemma: traditional project management methodologies—commonly referred to as "waterfall"—were failing. Projects were plagued by missed deadlines, ballooning costs, and solutions that no longer met customer needs by the time they were delivered. Something had to change.

The pivotal moment came in 2001 when a group of 17 forward-thinking software developers gathered in Snowbird, Utah. Frustrated with the inefficiencies of traditional methods, they crafted the **Agile Manifesto**, a groundbreaking document that would spark a revolution in project management and organizational behavior.

The Agile Manifesto: Principles That Changed the Game

The Agile Manifesto isn't just a set of principles; it's a mindset shift, a call to action to prioritize people over processes, and results over rigidity. It reads like a manifesto for freedom in work:

1. **Individuals and interactions over processes and tools.**

Agile prioritizes the power of collaboration. Tools and processes are important, but it's people who drive innovation and solve problems.

2. **Working software over comprehensive documentation.**
Traditional methods often prioritized paperwork over progress. Agile flips this on its head, emphasizing the delivery of tangible results.

3. **Customer collaboration over contract negotiation.**
Agile builds partnerships with customers, working with them to deliver what they truly need—not just what they initially thought they wanted.

4. **Responding to change over following a plan.**
In a fast-moving world, adaptability isn't just a nice-to-have—it's a survival skill. Agile embraces change as an opportunity, not a disruption.

These core principles are supported by 12 guiding practices, from delivering value frequently to fostering sustainable development. Together, they create a framework for high-performance work that can be applied far beyond software development.

The Benefits of Agile in Today's World

Agile is not just about improving processes; it's about transforming outcomes. Organizations that adopt Agile principles unlock a treasure trove of benefits:

1. Faster Delivery of Value

Agile is all about speed. By breaking work into smaller, manageable increments, teams can deliver value to customers sooner. Whether it's a working prototype or a fully finished feature, Agile ensures continuous progress.

2. Improved Quality and Reduced Waste

With its focus on frequent testing and iterative

refinement, Agile reduces defects and improves overall quality. Teams identify issues early and correct course, eliminating wasted effort and rework.

3. Greater Customer Satisfaction

Agile puts the customer at the heart of everything. Continuous feedback loops ensure that what's being delivered aligns with real needs, leading to higher satisfaction and loyalty.

4. Increased Team Morale and Productivity

Agile creates empowered teams that take ownership of their work. The emphasis on collaboration and transparency fosters trust, motivation, and a sense of purpose.

5. Resilience in a Changing World

The world is unpredictable, and businesses that can pivot quickly have a competitive edge. Agile's adaptive nature ensures that teams can respond to changes in priorities, market conditions, or customer demands with confidence.

Agile Isn't Just for Software: Expanding the Possibilities

While Agile originated in the software industry, its principles are universal. Today, Agile is being applied in industries as diverse as healthcare, finance, education, and manufacturing. Any organization that values speed, adaptability, and customer-centricity can harness the power of Agile to transform its operations and achieve extraordinary results.

Imagine a hospital using Agile to streamline patient care, a university applying Agile frameworks to curriculum development, or a marketing team delivering campaigns in sprints to maximize impact. The possibilities are endless.

Common Myths About Agile: Busting the Misconceptions

As transformative as Agile can be, it's often

misunderstood. Let's address some common myths:

1. **"Agile means no planning."** This couldn't be further from the truth. Agile involves constant planning—but unlike traditional methods, planning is iterative and flexible.

2. **"Agile is only for software teams."** As we've seen, Agile principles can be applied to any domain, from product development to operations and beyond.

3. **"Agile is chaotic."** Agile isn't about chaos; it's about control through adaptability. Agile teams operate with clear goals, structured workflows, and accountability.

4. **"Agile eliminates documentation."** Agile reduces unnecessary documentation but retains what's essential. The focus is on delivering value, not creating paperwork for its own sake.

What's Next: Diving Deeper Into Agile Frameworks

Now that we've explored what Agile is and why it matters, the next step is understanding the frameworks that bring Agile to life. Scrum, Kanban, and Lean are three of the most widely used frameworks, each offering unique strengths and strategies.

In the next chapter, we'll delve into these frameworks, helping you identify which one (or combination) is best suited for your team and organization. Remember, Agile isn't a one-size-fits-all solution—it's a philosophy that adapts to your needs, just as you adapt to your challenges.

Call to Action: Your Journey to Agile Excellence

Before we move forward, I challenge you to reflect: Where in your organization—or your life—could you benefit from being more Agile?

Whether it's delivering projects faster, improving collaboration, or simply embracing change with a positive mindset, the principles of Agile hold the key to unlocking your potential.

Remember, Agile is not just a process or a framework. It's a way of thinking, working, and achieving. So, as we continue this journey together, I encourage you to embrace the possibilities. Because when you master Agile, you don't just improve your team or your organization—you transform your future.

Let's get started.

Chapter 2 - Understanding Agile Frameworks

If Agile is the engine of innovation and adaptability, then Agile frameworks are its blueprints—detailed roadmaps that guide us on how to turn principles into action. Frameworks like Scrum, Kanban, and Lean have become cornerstones of Agile success, each offering unique tools, practices, and philosophies that empower teams to achieve extraordinary results. But here's the secret: the power of these frameworks lies not in rigidly following them, but in understanding their essence and tailoring them to your unique context.

In this chapter, we'll explore the three most influential Agile frameworks, compare their strengths, and introduce the concept of hybrid models like Lean-Agile. By the end, you'll have the knowledge to choose or customize a framework that's perfectly aligned with your goals and challenges.

Scrum: The Art of Sprints and Focus

Scrum is the poster child of Agile frameworks, and for good reason. Created by Jeff Sutherland and Ken Schwaber in the early 1990s, Scrum provides a lightweight yet powerful framework for managing complex projects. Its strength lies in its simplicity and focus: it breaks work into small, manageable increments called **sprints**, typically lasting two to four weeks.

At its core, Scrum is a framework designed to maximize team focus, collaboration, and adaptability. Its structured approach helps teams deliver value incrementally while maintaining the flexibility to respond to changing needs.

Key Components of Scrum

1. **The Scrum Roles**

    - **Scrum Master**: The guardian of the process, the Scrum Master ensures that the team adheres to Scrum principles while removing obstacles that hinder progress. Think of them as the coach who keeps the team in top form.

    - **Product Owner**: The visionary behind the product, the Product Owner prioritizes the work and ensures that the team is always delivering maximum value to stakeholders.

    - **Development Team**: A self-organizing group of professionals who bring the vision to life, the development team is the heart of Scrum.

2. **The Scrum Artifacts**

- **Product Backlog**: A prioritized list of everything that needs to be done for the product, from high-level features to detailed tasks.

- **Sprint Backlog**: A subset of the product backlog that the team commits to completing during the sprint.

- **Increment**: The tangible output of the sprint, a potentially shippable piece of work that adds value.

3. **The Scrum Events**

    - **Sprint Planning**: Teams set goals for the sprint and decide which backlog items they'll tackle.

    - **Daily Scrum**: A short, focused meeting where the team synchronizes and identifies any blockers.

    - **Sprint Review**: Stakeholders review the sprint's output and provide feedback.

- **Sprint Retrospective**: The team reflects on what went well, what didn't, and how they can improve.

Scrum thrives in environments where priorities shift frequently, and it excels at fostering transparency, accountability, and iterative improvement.

Kanban: The Power of Visualization

If Scrum is a structured sprint, Kanban is a steady flow. Originating from Lean manufacturing, Kanban emphasizes continuous delivery, visualizing workflows, and limiting work in progress (WIP) to improve efficiency.

The Principles of Kanban

1. **Start with what you do now.** Unlike Scrum, Kanban doesn't require teams to adopt a new process wholesale. Instead, it encourages incremental improvements to existing workflows.

2. **Visualize the workflow.** The Kanban board is the centerpiece of this framework. Tasks are represented as cards that move through columns representing different stages of work, from "To Do" to "Done."

3. **Limit work in progress (WIP).** By setting WIP limits, Kanban prevents teams from spreading themselves too thin, ensuring that focus and quality remain high.

4. **Manage flow.** Kanban helps teams identify bottlenecks and optimize the flow of work. This leads to faster delivery and greater predictability.

When to Use Kanban

Kanban is ideal for teams that require flexibility, such as operations or support teams, and for those seeking to improve processes without overhauling their current systems. Its continuous delivery model makes it perfect for environments with a steady stream of incoming tasks.

Lean: Delivering Value Without Waste

Lean is more than a framework—it's a philosophy rooted in maximizing value while minimizing waste. Popularized by Toyota in the mid-20th century, Lean principles have influenced not only Agile but countless other business methodologies.

The Core Principles of Lean

1. **Eliminate waste.**
   Waste can take many forms: unnecessary meetings, excessive documentation, or time spent on low-priority tasks. Lean helps teams focus on what truly matters.

2. **Amplify learning.**
   Lean encourages continuous experimentation and improvement, fostering an environment where teams learn from their successes and failures.

3. **Deliver as fast as possible.**
   By breaking work into small, deliverable

increments, Lean ensures rapid feedback and faster delivery.

4. **Empower the team.** Lean emphasizes respect for people, encouraging teams to take ownership of their work and collaborate effectively.

5. **Optimize the whole.** Rather than optimizing individual parts of a process, Lean looks at the big picture to ensure that every part of the organization contributes to overall success.

Lean in Agile

Lean's principles often overlap with Agile practices, making it a natural fit for organizations seeking to enhance efficiency and quality. While Lean is more of a mindset than a step-by-step framework, its emphasis on delivering value aligns perfectly with Agile goals.

Comparing Frameworks: Finding Your Fit

So, how do you decide which framework is right for your team? The answer depends on your goals, team dynamics, and the nature of your work. Let's compare Scrum, Kanban, and Lean:

Framework	Best For	Key Strengths	Potential Challenges
Scrum	Complex projects with changing priorities	Clear structure, iterative progress	Requires team discipline and commitment
Kanban	Continuous work streams	Flexibility, ease of implementation	Can lack structure for some teams
Lean	Broad organizational improvements	Focus on value, big-picture thinking	Requires a culture shift

Lean-Agile: The Best of Both Worlds

What if you don't have to choose just one framework? Enter **Lean-Agile**, a hybrid model that combines the structured adaptability of Agile with the efficiency and value-driven mindset of Lean.

Why Lean-Agile Works

Lean-Agile takes the best aspects of both philosophies: Agile's focus on customer collaboration and iterative delivery, and Lean's emphasis on eliminating waste and optimizing the whole. This hybrid approach is particularly effective in large organizations, where scaling Agile practices can be challenging.

Applying Lean-Agile in Practice

- **Aligning Teams:** Use Agile frameworks like Scrum or Kanban for individual teams, while applying Lean principles to ensure cross-team alignment.

- **Streamlining Value Streams:** Focus on delivering value to customers by optimizing workflows across the organization.

- **Fostering a Continuous Improvement Culture:** Encourage teams to experiment, measure results, and refine their processes over time.

Building Your Agile Toolkit

As you explore these frameworks, remember that Agile is not about dogma—it's about outcomes. You don't have to rigidly adhere to any one framework. Instead, use them as tools to achieve your goals. Experiment, adapt, and evolve.

Here's a pro tip: Involve your team in the decision-making process. When people feel ownership over how they work, they're more likely to commit to the journey. Agile isn't just something you implement—it's something you live and breathe as a team.

The Journey Ahead

Understanding Agile frameworks is like learning to navigate a map. You now have the knowledge to chart a course, but the real magic happens when you start the journey. In the next chapter, we'll dive into the Agile mindset—the psychological foundation that powers every successful Agile team. Because while frameworks are essential, it's the mindset behind them that truly drives excellence.

Let's take the next step. The adventure is just beginning.

Chapter 3 - The Agile Mindset

What separates a mediocre Agile team from a high-performing, unstoppable force? It's not just tools or frameworks—it's **mindset**. The Agile mindset is the foundation upon which every successful Agile practice is built. It's a way of thinking, behaving, and collaborating that enables individuals and teams to adapt, innovate, and thrive in the face of uncertainty.

Here's the truth: You can't "do Agile" without **being Agile**. The right mindset transforms Agile from a process into a culture, a movement, and, ultimately, a way of life. In this chapter, we'll explore what it means to cultivate an Agile mindset, how to foster a culture of continuous improvement, and why psychological safety is the secret ingredient for unlocking your team's potential.

What Is the Agile Mindset?

At its core, the Agile mindset is about **embracing change, fostering collaboration, and relentlessly pursuing excellence**. It's about focusing on outcomes over outputs, people over processes, and learning over perfection. The Agile Manifesto gave us the guiding principles, but the mindset breathes life into those principles.

Let's break it down into three fundamental pillars:

1. **Adaptability**
   Change isn't the enemy—it's the fuel for growth. An Agile mindset thrives in environments where priorities shift, obstacles emerge, and the unknown looms large. It's about saying, "Bring it on!" instead of resisting.

2. **Collaboration**
   No one succeeds alone in Agile. The mindset champions collective intelligence, where diverse perspectives converge to create better solutions. This requires not just working together but truly **aligning around shared goals**.

3. **Continuous Improvement**
   Agile teams are never satisfied with "good enough." They constantly seek ways to get better, whether through feedback loops, retrospectives, or bold experimentation. Growth isn't an event—it's a daily commitment.

Cultivating an Agile Culture

If mindset is the seed, culture is the soil. Your organization's culture determines whether the Agile mindset flourishes or withers. Here's how to create an environment where Agile thinking thrives.

1. Lead with Purpose

People don't rally around tasks; they rally around meaning. Leaders must articulate a clear, compelling purpose that connects every team member to the organization's larger mission. Why does this work matter? Who benefits? What's at stake?

When your team understands the "why" behind their work, they're not just following a process—they're part of a movement. Purpose fuels passion, and passion drives performance.

2. Empower Teams

Micromanagement kills the Agile mindset faster than anything else. To cultivate autonomy, trust your teams to make decisions, solve problems, and own their outcomes. Empowerment isn't about relinquishing control—it's about unleashing potential.

Empowered teams are more creative, more engaged, and more accountable. They don't wait for permission to innovate—they make it happen.

3. Foster a Feedback-Rich Environment

Feedback isn't criticism—it's a gift. High-performing Agile teams treat feedback as a superpower, using it to learn, adapt, and improve. Create rituals that make feedback a natural part of your culture, from retrospective meetings to one-on-one check-ins.

But here's the catch: Feedback must be **constructive, timely, and actionable**. It's not about blame; it's about better.

4. Celebrate Failure as Learning

In Agile, failure isn't the opposite of success—it's a step on the path to success. Cultivate a culture where experimentation is encouraged, and failure is viewed as an opportunity to learn. This doesn't mean tolerating carelessness; it means rewarding courage and curiosity.

The Role of Psychological Safety in Agile Teams

Imagine a workplace where people feel safe to

speak up, share ideas, and take risks without fear of ridicule or retribution. That's psychological safety, and it's the backbone of the Agile mindset.

Why Psychological Safety Matters

Without psychological safety, team members hold back. They hesitate to voice concerns, challenge assumptions, or propose bold ideas. This stifles innovation and collaboration, two pillars of Agile success.

Teams with high psychological safety, on the other hand, are unstoppable. They communicate openly, experiment fearlessly, and support each other through challenges. In these environments, problems are solved faster, and trust becomes the norm.

How to Build Psychological Safety

1. **Model Vulnerability as a Leader** Leaders set the tone. Share your own challenges, admit mistakes, and invite feedback. When leaders are vulnerable, they give permission for others to do the same.

2. **Encourage Radical Candor**
   Honest conversations are the cornerstone of psychological safety. Teach your team how to give and receive feedback with respect and care. Candor should be direct, but never cruel.

3. **Prioritize Inclusivity**
   Diversity of thought fuels innovation, but only if everyone feels heard. Create spaces where every voice matters, and actively seek out perspectives that challenge the status quo.

4. **Focus on Solutions, Not Blame**
   When mistakes happen—and they will—shift the conversation from "Who's at fault?" to "What can we learn?" Blame creates fear; solutions create progress.

Embracing Continuous Improvement

Continuous improvement isn't a goal—it's a habit. Agile teams are relentless about getting better, not just in their work but in how they work.

The Kaizen Philosophy

Borrowed from Lean principles, **Kaizen** is the Japanese concept of continuous, incremental improvement. It's about making small changes every day that lead to big results over time.

In Agile, Kaizen manifests through practices like retrospectives, where teams analyze their performance and commit to one or two areas of improvement. The magic lies in the **cumulative effect**: small gains compound into extraordinary progress.

Tools for Continuous Improvement

1. **Retrospectives**
   The retrospective is a sacred Agile ritual. It's where teams pause to reflect on what's working, what's not, and how they can improve. Keep these sessions focused, honest, and action-oriented.

2. **Metrics and Dashboards**

You can't improve what you don't measure. Use metrics like velocity, cycle time, and customer satisfaction to track progress and identify bottlenecks. Just remember: metrics are a compass, not a scorecard.

3. **Experimentation**
   Agile teams aren't afraid to try new approaches, even if they don't always work. Encourage experimentation by setting clear hypotheses, testing small changes, and analyzing results.

Case Study: The Power of Mindset

Let me share a story about a team that transformed through the Agile mindset. At first, they were bogged down by rigid processes, siloed thinking, and a fear of failure. Deadlines were missed, morale was low, and innovation was nonexistent.

But everything changed when they embraced the Agile mindset. They started with small steps:

creating a safe space for honest feedback, empowering team members to make decisions, and celebrating wins—no matter how small. Over time, their culture shifted. Collaboration replaced competition. Experimentation replaced caution. And success replaced stagnation.

Within six months, their productivity skyrocketed, employee satisfaction soared, and they delivered a groundbreaking product ahead of schedule. The secret wasn't just Agile practices—it was Agile thinking.

Bringing It All Together

The Agile mindset isn't a switch you flip—it's a muscle you build. It requires intention, practice, and commitment. But the rewards are worth it: teams that are more resilient, innovative, and aligned than ever before.

Here's your challenge: Take one concept from this chapter and apply it to your team today. Maybe it's creating a feedback loop, empowering a team member, or leading with vulnerability. Whatever it is, start small but think big. The Agile mindset is your most powerful tool for transformation.

In the next chapter, we'll explore how to put this mindset into action through Agile project management essentials. Get ready to bridge the gap between thinking and doing—because your Agile journey is just beginning.

Chapter 4 - Agile Project Management Essentials

In the traditional world of project management, everything was about control: rigid timelines, fixed budgets, and detailed plans etched in stone. But the world has changed. Today, uncertainty is the norm, not the exception. Markets shift overnight, customer needs evolve, and technology accelerates faster than we can blink.

Enter **Agile project management**, a revolution in how we approach work. It's not about controlling chaos; it's about thriving in it. Agile project management is about creating value in short cycles, embracing change, and delivering results that matter.

In this chapter, we'll unpack what makes Agile project management a game-changer. We'll dive into how it differs from traditional approaches, explore the core principles driving its success, and equip you with practical tools to manage scope, time, and cost in a way that's dynamic, adaptive, and effective.

The Shift from Traditional to Agile Project Management

Let's start with a truth that most organizations struggle to accept: **the old way doesn't work anymore**. Traditional project management relies on assumptions of predictability. It treats projects as linear journeys—plan the work, work the plan, and voilà, success! But what happens when reality deviates from the plan?

In the Agile world, we embrace the unpredictable. Agile project management acknowledges that plans will change, priorities will shift, and obstacles will arise. The key is to remain flexible, responsive, and customer-focused.

The Waterfall vs. Agile Paradigm

Traditional project management, often called the **Waterfall model**, operates like a cascading sequence of steps:

1. Requirements gathering
2. Design
3. Implementation
4. Testing
5. Delivery

Each phase is dependent on the previous one, and there's little room to pivot once the project is underway.

Agile flips this script. Instead of a long, linear process, Agile delivers work in small, incremental cycles called **iterations** or **sprints**. Each sprint produces a usable product or feature, enabling teams to gather feedback and adapt before moving forward.

The results? **Speed, flexibility, and customer satisfaction**. Agile doesn't just manage change—it leverages it as a competitive advantage.

Managing Scope, Time, and Cost the Agile Way

In traditional project management, scope, time, and cost are treated as fixed constraints. Change one, and the entire project might collapse like a house of cards. Agile, however, views these elements as interdependent levers that can flex to maximize value.

1. Scope Management

Traditional thinking says, "Define the scope up front and stick to it." But how often do customers know exactly what they want at the beginning of a project? Rarely. Agile embraces **evolving scope** through continuous collaboration with stakeholders.

- **Prioritize ruthlessly**: Agile teams use tools like the **product backlog** to rank features by value. The most critical work gets done first, ensuring that even if the project ends early, the highest-priority items are delivered.

- **Welcome change**: Agile thrives on adaptability. Changes to scope aren't failures—they're opportunities to align with what customers truly need.

2. Time Management

In Agile, time is a fixed constraint. Each sprint operates within a set timebox, typically two to four weeks. This creates urgency, focus, and discipline.

- **Break work into manageable chunks**: Instead of tackling massive tasks, Agile teams divide work into smaller, actionable items. This ensures progress is visible and momentum builds.

- **Iterate for speed**: By delivering in increments, Agile teams can release value faster and respond to feedback immediately.

3. Cost Management

Agile teams manage cost by controlling the time and resources allocated to each sprint. This prevents runaway budgets and ensures every dollar delivers value.

- **Focus on ROI**: Agile prioritizes high-impact work that delivers the greatest return on investment.

- **Transparency drives efficiency**: Frequent reviews and retrospectives ensure that budgets are spent wisely, with inefficiencies identified and eliminated quickly.

Iterative Planning and Delivery

Planning in Agile isn't a one-and-done event. It's a dynamic, ongoing process that evolves as the project progresses.

1. Sprint Planning

At the start of each sprint, the team holds a **sprint**

planning session to:

- Select items from the product backlog.
- Define the sprint goal.
- Break tasks into manageable units of work.

The result? A clear, actionable plan that aligns the team and sets the stage for success.

2. Daily Standups

Every day, Agile teams hold **standup meetings** to discuss three key questions:

1. What did I accomplish yesterday?
2. What will I work on today?
3. Are there any blockers?

These quick, focused check-ins keep everyone aligned and allow teams to address issues before they derail progress.

3. Iterative Delivery

At the end of each sprint, teams deliver a working product or feature. This isn't a half-baked prototype—it's something tangible, valuable, and usable. By delivering iteratively, Agile teams reduce risk, gather feedback, and ensure they're always moving in the right direction.

Tools and Techniques for Agile Project Management

Agile project management is as much about mindset as it is about mechanics. To bring it to life, teams rely on a suite of tools and techniques that streamline workflows, enhance communication, and deliver results.

1. User Stories

Agile teams use **user stories** to capture requirements in plain, human language. A user story typically follows this format: "As a [user], I want [goal] so that [benefit]."

This keeps the focus on delivering value to the end user, not just ticking off tasks.

2. Task Boards

Tools like physical task boards or digital platforms (e.g., Trello, Jira, or Asana) help teams visualize their work. Tasks move through columns like **To Do**, **In Progress**, and **Done**, providing real-time visibility into the team's progress.

3. Burndown Charts

A **burndown chart** tracks how much work remains in a sprint. It's a simple yet powerful way to monitor progress and ensure the team stays on track.

Overcoming Common Challenges

Agile project management isn't without its hurdles. Here are some common challenges—and how to overcome them:

Challenge 1: Scope Creep

When stakeholders keep adding features, it's easy for projects to spiral out of control. Agile combats this by:

- Prioritizing work in the product backlog.
- Clearly defining sprint goals.
- Educating stakeholders on the importance of focus.

Challenge 2: Team Misalignment

Misaligned teams waste time and energy. To ensure alignment:

- Hold regular standups.
- Establish a shared sprint goal.
- Use transparent task boards to keep everyone on the same page.

Challenge 3: Resistance to Change

Some people cling to old ways of working. Overcome resistance by:

- Demonstrating quick wins.
- Providing training and support.
- Celebrating successes to build momentum.

Bringing It All Together

Agile project management isn't just a method—it's a mindset and a movement. By embracing iterative planning, adaptive scope, and dynamic delivery, you'll unlock the full potential of your team and deliver results that truly matter.

The journey isn't always easy, but the rewards are immense. Take the first step by applying one Agile principle to your next project. Whether it's holding a standup, prioritizing a backlog, or running a retrospective, every small change brings you closer to Agile excellence.

Next, we'll dive into the **roles that drive Agile success**—from Scrum Masters to Product Owners to Agile Coaches. Get ready to build self-organizing teams that are empowered, energized, and unstoppable.

Chapter 5 - Roles in Agile Teams

Agile teams are like high-performing sports teams: everyone has a role to play, and success depends on seamless collaboration. In this chapter, we'll dive deep into the key roles that drive Agile excellence—roles designed not to control but to empower teams to adapt, innovate, and deliver.

We'll explore the responsibilities of the **Scrum Master**, the **Product Owner**, and the **Agile Coach**, as well as the dynamics of self-organizing, cross-functional teams. And most importantly, we'll unpack what it means to lead in Agile: how to guide without micromanaging, inspire without dictating, and foster an environment where people do their best work.

The Core Pillars of Agile Roles

In Agile, roles aren't about hierarchy; they're about function. Every role exists to support the team in delivering value. Whether it's clearing roadblocks, prioritizing work, or facilitating collaboration, the focus is on enabling the team—not controlling it.

Unlike traditional top-down structures, Agile encourages **shared ownership and accountability**. This means every team member contributes to the success of the project, not just the leaders. It's this collective responsibility that creates an environment where innovation and high performance thrive.

The Three Pillars: Leadership, Ownership, and Execution

1. **Leadership**: Agile leadership is about creating conditions for success. Leaders don't command from the top—they serve from within.

2. **Ownership**: In Agile, individuals take full ownership of their work. They're empowered to make decisions and held accountable for their outcomes.

3. **Execution**: Agile teams focus on doing, iterating, and improving. Execution is driven by a commitment to continuous learning and delivering value.

The Scrum Master: The Guardian of Flow

The **Scrum Master** is often misunderstood. They're not a manager or a taskmaster—they're a servant leader, a coach, and a catalyst for team performance.

Responsibilities of the Scrum Master

1. **Facilitating Scrum Events**
   The Scrum Master ensures that Scrum ceremonies—like sprint planning, daily standups, sprint reviews, and retrospectives—happen smoothly and

effectively. These events aren't just rituals; they're opportunities for alignment, problem-solving, and growth.

2. **Removing Obstacles**
Roadblocks are inevitable. Whether it's a technical issue, a process bottleneck, or team friction, the Scrum Master's job is to clear the path so the team can focus on delivering value.

3. **Coaching the Team**
The Scrum Master helps the team embrace Agile principles and practices. They coach individuals to self-organize, collaborate, and continuously improve.

4. **Shielding the Team**
Distractions and interruptions can derail progress. The Scrum Master acts as a buffer, protecting the team from unnecessary meetings, conflicting priorities, and outside noise.

The Scrum Master's Secret Weapon: Servant

Leadership

Servant leadership is the heart of the Scrum Master's role. It's about empowering the team rather than exerting authority. By putting the team's needs first, the Scrum Master creates a culture of trust, collaboration, and high performance.

The Product Owner: The Voice of the Customer

If the Scrum Master is the guardian of flow, the **Product Owner** is the guardian of value. They represent the customer and ensure the team is always working on the right things at the right time.

Responsibilities of the Product Owner

1. **Defining and Prioritizing the Backlog**
   The product backlog is the heart of Agile development. The Product Owner is responsible for maintaining it—defining user stories, prioritizing features, and ensuring

that every item aligns with the project's goals.

2. **Communicating the Vision**
A clear vision is essential for guiding the team. The Product Owner paints a vivid picture of what success looks like and aligns the team around it.

3. **Collaborating with Stakeholders**
The Product Owner serves as the bridge between the team and stakeholders. They gather input, manage expectations, and ensure everyone is aligned.

4. **Making Tough Decisions**
Trade-offs are inevitable in any project. The Product Owner must decide what to prioritize, what to defer, and what to eliminate—all while keeping the customer's needs front and center.

The Product Owner's Secret Weapon: Strategic Thinking

Great Product Owners are strategic thinkers. They

don't just react to requests—they anticipate needs, analyze trade-offs, and make decisions that maximize value.

The Agile Coach: The Architect of Growth

While the Scrum Master focuses on the team, the **Agile Coach** takes a broader view. They work across teams, departments, and sometimes the entire organization to foster an Agile culture.

Responsibilities of the Agile Coach

1. **Driving Agile Adoption**
   The Agile Coach helps teams and organizations adopt Agile practices, principles, and mindsets. They provide training, guidance, and support to ensure successful implementation.

2. **Facilitating Change**
   Agile transformation is a journey, not an event. The Agile Coach guides organizations through this journey, addressing resistance,

fostering collaboration, and aligning efforts.

3. **Building Capability**
The goal of the Agile Coach isn't to create dependency—it's to build capability. They mentor leaders, train teams, and develop processes that enable long-term success.

4. **Promoting Continuous Improvement**
The Agile Coach helps organizations embrace a culture of continuous improvement. Whether it's refining processes, enhancing collaboration, or optimizing delivery, they're always pushing for better.

The Agile Coach's Secret Weapon: Emotional Intelligence

Agile transformation is as much about people as it is about processes. Great Agile Coaches have high emotional intelligence. They understand the fears, motivations, and dynamics of teams and use this insight to drive change.

Building Self-Organizing, Cross-Functional Teams

In Agile, the team is the engine of success. But not just any team—a **self-organizing, cross-functional team**. This means:

- **Self-organizing**: The team decides how to tackle work, without relying on micromanagement.

- **Cross-functional**: The team has all the skills needed to deliver value, from design to development to testing.

The Dynamics of High-Performing Teams

1. **Shared Purpose**
   High-performing teams are united by a common goal. They understand the "why" behind their work and are committed to achieving it.

2. **Collaboration and Trust**
   Agile thrives on collaboration. Teams must trust each other, communicate openly, and work together to solve problems.

3. **Accountability**

   In Agile, accountability is shared. Team members take ownership of their work and hold each other accountable for delivering results.

4. **Adaptability**

   Agile teams are flexible. They embrace change, experiment with new ideas, and adapt to feedback.

Leadership in Agile: Guiding Without Micromanaging

Leadership in Agile is a balancing act. It's about guiding the team without controlling them, inspiring without dictating, and enabling without interfering.

The Traits of an Agile Leader

1. **Empathy**

   Agile leaders understand their team's needs, motivations, and challenges. They lead with empathy, creating an environment of psychological safety.

2. **Vision**

   Agile leaders provide clarity and direction. They articulate a compelling vision that inspires the team and aligns efforts.

3. **Humility**

   Agile leaders don't have all the answers—and they're okay with that. They listen, learn, and empower their teams to find the best solutions.

4. **Adaptability**

   Agile leaders embrace change. They're flexible, open-minded, and willing to pivot when necessary.

The Art of Empowerment

Empowerment is the cornerstone of Agile leadership. It's about giving people the freedom to make decisions, experiment, and take ownership of their work. When teams feel empowered, they're more engaged, innovative, and committed to success.

Bringing It All Together

Agile roles are more than job titles—they're functions designed to support the team and deliver value. Whether you're a Scrum Master, Product Owner, Agile Coach, or team member, your role is critical to the success of the project.

But remember, Agile isn't about rigid roles or strict hierarchies. It's about collaboration, adaptability, and shared ownership. By embracing these principles, you'll create teams that are empowered, aligned, and unstoppable.

Next, we'll explore the **core practices that drive Agile excellence**—from sprints and standups to Kanban boards and Lean principles. Get ready to dive into the mechanics of Agile and take your team's performance to the next level.

Chapter 6 - Core Practices for Agile Excellence

Practices are the heartbeat of Agile. They're the tangible actions that bring Agile principles to life, the rituals and habits that create momentum and drive results. But here's the key: Agile practices aren't about following a rigid formula—they're about creating a framework where adaptability, innovation, and collaboration thrive.

In this chapter, we'll unpack the core practices that power Agile excellence. From Scrum's sprints, backlogs, and stand-ups, to Kanban's visual workflows and Lean's relentless focus on value, these practices are your toolkit for building high-performing teams and delivering extraordinary results.

Sprints: The Engine of Iterative Progress

At the heart of Scrum is the sprint—a time-boxed period (usually 1–4 weeks) where the team focuses on delivering a specific, incremental set of work. Sprints are about creating rhythm and focus, driving the team toward tangible outcomes in manageable, iterative chunks.

Why Sprints Work

1. **Focus on Priorities**
   By committing to a specific set of tasks for the sprint, the team eliminates distractions and focuses on what matters most.

2. **Frequent Feedback Loops**
   Each sprint ends with a deliverable that stakeholders can review. This ensures the team is always aligned with the customer's needs.

3. **Continuous Improvement**

Sprints create natural checkpoints for reflection. Retrospectives allow the team to identify what's working, what's not, and how to improve.

The Sprint Lifecycle

1. **Sprint Planning**
Sprint planning is where it all begins. The team collaborates to decide what work will be completed during the sprint. This includes selecting items from the backlog, defining the sprint goal, and breaking down tasks into manageable pieces.

2. **The Sprint**
During the sprint, the team focuses on executing the plan. Daily stand-ups keep everyone aligned, identify roadblocks, and foster collaboration.

3. **Sprint Review**
At the end of the sprint, the team showcases their work to stakeholders. This is a chance to gather feedback, celebrate achievements,

and align on next steps.

4. **Sprint Retrospective**

   The retrospective is the team's opportunity to reflect on their performance. What went well? What could be better? This ritual is key to fostering a culture of continuous improvement.

Backlogs: The Blueprint for Success

The backlog is the single source of truth for Agile teams. It's a dynamic, prioritized list of work that evolves based on feedback, changing priorities, and new insights.

The Product Backlog

The product backlog is owned by the Product Owner and represents the team's to-do list. It's more than a collection of tasks—it's a strategic tool for delivering value.

1. **User Stories**

   User stories are the building blocks of the

backlog. They describe what the user needs, why they need it, and how it creates value. *Example:* "As a customer, I want to filter products by price, so I can find options within my budget."

2. **Prioritization**

   Not all work is created equal. The Product Owner prioritizes the backlog to ensure the team is always working on the most valuable items.

3. **Refinement**

   Backlog refinement is an ongoing process. The team collaborates to clarify, estimate, and update backlog items, ensuring they're ready for the next sprint.

The Sprint Backlog

The sprint backlog is a subset of the product backlog. It contains the items the team commits to completing during the sprint. It's the team's tactical plan for achieving the sprint goal.

Stand-Ups: The Pulse of the Team

The daily stand-up is a short, focused meeting where the team aligns on progress, identifies roadblocks, and plans for the day. It's not just a status update—it's a tool for fostering communication, accountability, and collaboration.

The Three Key Questions

1. **What did you accomplish yesterday?**
2. **What will you work on today?**
3. **What obstacles are in your way?**

By answering these questions, the team gains a clear understanding of where they stand and how they can support each other.

Best Practices for Stand-Ups

- **Keep it Short**: Aim for 15 minutes or less.
- **Stay Focused**: Avoid diving into detailed discussions. Save those for after the stand-up.

- **Encourage Participation**: Everyone on the team should contribute.

Visualizing Workflows with Kanban

Kanban is all about visibility. By visualizing the team's workflow on a Kanban board, everyone can see what's in progress, what's done, and what's coming next.

The Power of Kanban

1. **Transparency**
   A Kanban board makes work visible to everyone. This fosters accountability and helps the team stay aligned.

2. **Work in Progress (WIP) Limits**
   Kanban encourages teams to limit the number of tasks in progress. This reduces context switching, improves focus, and accelerates delivery.

3. **Continuous Flow**
   Unlike Scrum, which operates in time-boxed

sprints, Kanban focuses on maintaining a steady flow of work.

Setting Up a Kanban Board

A typical Kanban board has three columns:

- **To Do**: Tasks waiting to be started.
- **In Progress**: Tasks currently being worked on.
- **Done**: Completed tasks.

Teams can customize their board to fit their workflow, adding columns like "Review" or "Testing" as needed.

Streamlining Value Delivery with Lean Practices

Lean is the foundation of Agile. It's a mindset and a methodology for delivering maximum value with minimal waste. By focusing on efficiency, quality, and customer value, Lean practices amplify the impact of Agile teams.

The Principles of Lean

1. **Value**
   Identify what creates value for the customer and focus efforts on delivering it.

2. **Flow**
   Streamline processes to ensure work flows smoothly and efficiently.

3. **Pull**
   Work is "pulled" based on demand, rather than being "pushed" through a fixed schedule.

4. **Continuous Improvement**
   Lean teams are relentless in their pursuit of better ways to work.

Applying Lean to Agile Practices

- **Value Stream Mapping**
  Analyze the flow of work from start to finish, identifying bottlenecks and opportunities for improvement.

- **Eliminating Waste**

Challenge every step in your process. If it doesn't add value, eliminate it.

- **Optimizing Batch Size**
  Work on smaller batches to reduce risk, improve quality, and deliver faster.

Integrating Practices for Maximum Impact

The magic of Agile practices lies in how they integrate. Sprints drive focus and rhythm. Backlogs ensure alignment and prioritization. Stand-ups foster collaboration. Kanban visualizes workflows. And Lean principles maximize value.

Customizing Practices for Your Team

Every team is unique. What works for one may not work for another. The key is to experiment, adapt, and refine practices to fit your team's needs and goals.

Creating a Culture of Execution

Practices are only as effective as the culture they're built on. Agile teams thrive when they embrace a culture of execution—where taking action, delivering results, and learning from experience are core values.

1. **Set Clear Goals**
   Teams perform best when they know what they're working toward. Clear, measurable goals create focus and drive.

2. **Empower Decision-Making**
   Give teams the autonomy to make decisions. This fosters accountability and accelerates progress.

3. **Celebrate Wins**
   Recognize and celebrate achievements—big and small. This boosts morale and reinforces positive behaviors.

The Journey to Agile Excellence

Mastering Agile practices is a journey, not a

destination. As your team adopts and refines these practices, you'll see them evolve into a high-performing, adaptable, and resilient unit.

In the next chapter, we'll explore how to embed **quality control and continuous improvement** into every aspect of Agile. Because excellence isn't just about doing—it's about doing better every single day. Get ready to take your team to the next level.

Chapter 7 - Quality Control and Continuous Improvement

When it comes to Agile, delivering value is non-negotiable—but delivering quality is what separates good teams from great ones. Think about it: Would you rather get a product fast, only to find it riddled with errors and gaps, or receive something polished, effective, and reliable? In Agile, quality isn't just a step in the process—it's baked into everything the team does.

The beauty of Agile is its focus on adaptability and learning, and that's exactly what quality control and continuous improvement are about. They're not just technical practices; they're a mindset—a commitment to being better today than you were yesterday, every single day.

Embedding Quality into Agile Processes

Quality in Agile doesn't happen by accident. It's the result of intentional processes, rigorous practices, and a relentless commitment to excellence. In traditional project management, quality control might happen after the product is built. In Agile, it happens throughout the entire development process.

Shift Left: Moving Quality Upstream

The old-school approach to quality was reactive: test it after it's built, fix what's broken. Agile flips the script with the concept of "shifting left." By addressing quality early and often, you catch issues before they snowball into costly problems.

Here's how shifting left works in practice:

1. **Collaborative Requirements Gathering** Involve the entire team in defining

requirements. Engineers, testers, and stakeholders all contribute to creating user stories and acceptance criteria. This ensures clarity and alignment from the start.

2. **Definition of Done**
What does "done" mean for your team? In Agile, it's not just about completing a task; it's about meeting clear, agreed-upon quality standards. The Definition of Done might include:

    - Code reviewed and approved.

    - Unit tests written and passing.

    - Integrated into the main branch with no conflicts.

3. **Automated Testing from Day One**
The earlier you write automated tests, the faster you can identify bugs and ensure quality. We'll dive deeper into testing strategies later in this chapter.

Feedback Loops: The Lifeblood of Continuous Improvement

One of Agile's superpowers is its focus on feedback loops. Feedback is how you learn, adapt, and get better. It's how you ensure the product you're building is the product your customer actually needs.

Feedback Within the Team

Agile teams thrive on open communication and trust. Regular feedback—whether it's in retrospectives, code reviews, or informal check-ins—is how teams stay aligned and continuously improve.

1. **Daily Stand-Ups**
   Use stand-ups not just to report progress, but to surface obstacles and seek help. If something's not working, address it immediately.

2. **Sprint Retrospectives**
   The sprint retrospective is one of the most powerful feedback loops in Agile. It's a

chance to reflect on what went well, what didn't, and how the team can improve. Don't just go through the motions—make retrospectives a safe space for honest, actionable insights.

3. **Peer Reviews**

    Code reviews, design critiques, and pair programming sessions help ensure quality and foster learning. Constructive feedback from peers is an incredible accelerator for both individual and team growth.

Feedback From Stakeholders

The closer you are to your customers, the better your product will be. Agile embraces this by building stakeholder feedback into the process.

1. **Sprint Reviews**

    Sprint reviews aren't just for showing off completed work—they're for learning. Engage stakeholders in meaningful conversations about what you delivered. What works? What doesn't? What should you prioritize next?

2. **Usability Testing**

   Invite real users to test your product early and often. Their feedback can reveal gaps in understanding, unmet needs, or opportunities for innovation.

Testing Strategies in Agile

Testing in Agile isn't a phase; it's a mindset. It's something the entire team owns, from developers to testers to product owners. Effective testing ensures quality while enabling the team to move fast and confidently.

Automated Testing

Automation is the backbone of Agile testing. By automating repetitive and time-consuming tests, teams free up time to focus on what really matters: delivering value.

1. **Unit Testing**

   Unit tests validate individual components or

functions of your code. They're the foundation of a reliable codebase and are usually written by developers.

2. **Integration Testing**
Integration tests ensure that different parts of your application work together as expected. They catch issues that unit tests might miss.

3. **End-to-End Testing**
End-to-end tests simulate real user interactions, validating the system as a whole. These tests are slower and more complex, so use them sparingly for critical workflows.

4. **Continuous Integration and Continuous Deployment (CI/CD)**
A strong CI/CD pipeline integrates automated testing into the development process. Every time code is committed, tests run automatically, catching issues early.

Exploratory Testing

While automated tests handle predictable scenarios, exploratory testing is about uncovering the unexpected. Testers use their creativity and intuition to find edge cases, usability issues, and potential failures.

Regression Testing

Every change to your codebase introduces risk. Regression testing ensures new features or fixes don't break existing functionality. Automated regression suites are invaluable for maintaining confidence in your code.

Quality as a Team Responsibility

In traditional workflows, quality was often seen as the tester's job. Agile shifts that mindset. In a high-performing Agile team, **everyone** owns quality.

1. **Developers**
   Write clean, maintainable code. Follow best practices like Test-Driven Development (TDD) and pair programming.

2. **Testers**
   Go beyond finding bugs—be an advocate for the user. Collaborate with developers to create comprehensive test strategies.

3. **Product Owners**
   Define clear acceptance criteria. Ensure user stories reflect customer needs and include quality requirements.

4. **Scrum Masters**
   Facilitate discussions about quality during stand-ups, sprint reviews, and retrospectives. Remove obstacles that prevent the team from delivering high-quality work.

Continuous Improvement: The Kaizen Mindset

Kaizen, a Japanese term meaning "continuous improvement," is a core principle of both Lean and Agile. It's about making incremental changes every day to become more effective, efficient, and aligned with your goals.

How to Cultivate Continuous Improvement

1. **Retrospectives with a Purpose**
   Don't just identify issues—commit to action. Choose one or two concrete improvements to implement in the next sprint.

2. **Data-Driven Decision Making**
   Use metrics like cycle time, lead time, and defect rates to identify bottlenecks and track progress.

3. **Celebrate Wins and Learn From Failures**
   Acknowledge achievements and analyze mistakes without blame. Every experience is an opportunity to learn.

4. **Empower Experimentation**
   Encourage the team to try new tools, techniques, and approaches. Not every experiment will succeed, but the insights you gain will drive growth.

Tools for Quality and Improvement

There's no shortage of tools to help Agile teams embed quality and drive continuous improvement.

Testing Tools

1. **Selenium**

   Automate browser-based testing for web applications.

2. **JUnit/NUnit**

   Popular frameworks for unit testing in Java and .NET, respectively.

3. **Postman**

   Streamline API testing and automate test suites for backend systems.

Feedback Tools

1. **Jira**

   Track progress, manage backlogs, and visualize workflows.

2. **Miro**

   Facilitate collaborative retrospectives and brainstorming sessions.

3. **SurveyMonkey**

   Gather feedback from users and stakeholders.

CI/CD Tools

1. **Jenkins**

   Automate builds, testing, and deployment.

2. **GitLab CI/CD**

   Streamline version control and CI/CD pipelines.

3. **CircleCI**

   Run automated tests and deployments in the cloud.

Overcoming Challenges in Quality and Improvement

Even the best teams face obstacles on the road to quality and continuous improvement. Here's how to tackle some common challenges:

Resistance to Change

People are creatures of habit. Change can feel uncomfortable, even threatening. The key is to frame improvement as an opportunity, not a critique. Highlight the benefits of new practices, and involve the team in the decision-making process.

Balancing Speed and Quality

In the rush to deliver, quality can sometimes take a backseat. Remember: fast is slow without quality. Invest in practices like automated testing and CI/CD to maintain speed **and** quality.

Keeping Momentum

Continuous improvement isn't a one-time event—it's a way of life. Keep the momentum going by celebrating progress, revisiting goals, and staying curious.

The Agile Commitment to Excellence

Quality control and continuous improvement are more than just practices—they're a promise. A promise to your customers that you'll deliver value they can rely on. A promise to your team that you'll create an environment where they can do their best work. And a promise to yourself that you'll never settle for "good enough."

By embedding quality into every step of your process, leveraging feedback loops, and embracing a Kaizen mindset, you'll unlock the full potential of Agile.

In the next chapter, we'll shift our focus to the big picture: **starting your Agile transformation journey.** Whether you're building a team from scratch or guiding an established organization through change, we'll give you the roadmap to make it happen. Let's transform vision into action!

Chapter 8 - Starting the Agile Journey

Every transformation begins with a single step—but in Agile, that step is deliberate, calculated, and fueled by a clear vision. The Agile journey is not about blindly following frameworks or chasing trends. It's about embracing change, committing to excellence, and creating an environment where teams and organizations can thrive in a world that demands adaptability.

This chapter is your blueprint for starting strong. We'll explore how to assess your readiness, craft a roadmap for change, and align stakeholders behind a shared vision. Ready to launch? Let's dive in.

Assessing Readiness: Are You Ready for Agile?

Transformation doesn't happen in a vacuum. Before you dive headfirst into Agile, take a moment to assess where you stand. This isn't just about evaluating your processes or tools—it's about understanding your people, culture, and mindset.

Culture Check: Is Your Organization Ready to Adapt?

Agile isn't just a set of practices; it's a mindset. A culture that values collaboration, transparency, and continuous improvement is fertile ground for Agile to flourish. But what if your culture isn't there yet?

Ask yourself:

- **Do teams feel safe to fail?** Agile thrives on experimentation, which means failure must be seen as a stepping stone to success.

- **Are silos preventing collaboration?** Agile demands cross-functional teams that work together seamlessly.

- **Is leadership ready to trust and empower teams?** Micromanagement kills agility. Leaders must be willing to guide without controlling.

If your answers reveal gaps, don't worry—awareness is the first step toward change.

Process and Tools Assessment

Take stock of your current processes and tools. Are they enabling agility, or are they holding you back? Look for bottlenecks, inefficiencies, and outdated practices.

Examples of questions to ask:

- Are workflows clearly defined and visible to the team?

- Do you have mechanisms in place for regular feedback and iteration?

- Are your tools flexible enough to support Agile practices like backlogs, sprints, and kanban boards?

This isn't about overhauling everything overnight. It's about identifying where small, targeted changes can make the biggest impact.

Team Readiness

Agile teams are the heart of any transformation. Assess their readiness by considering:

- **Skills:** Do team members have the technical and collaborative skills to thrive in an Agile environment?

- **Mindset:** Are they open to change, or resistant?

- **Capacity:** Are teams overwhelmed with work, or do they have the bandwidth to take on a new way of working?

Crafting a Roadmap for Change

Now that you've assessed where you are, it's time to chart a path forward. A roadmap is more than just a timeline—it's a strategic guide that aligns efforts, resources, and goals.

Define Your Vision

Every great journey starts with a clear destination. What does success look like for your Agile transformation? Be specific.

Examples of vision statements:

- "Increase customer satisfaction by delivering valuable features every two weeks."
- "Empower teams to own their processes and collaborate effectively across departments."
- "Achieve faster time-to-market by reducing delivery cycle times by 30%."

A compelling vision inspires action. Make sure it's communicated clearly and often.

Set Achievable Milestones

Agile transformations don't happen all at once.

Break your journey into manageable milestones that build on each other.

For example:

1. Form an Agile pilot team to test new practices.
2. Train leadership and teams on Agile principles and frameworks.
3. Roll out Scrum practices, starting with sprint planning and retrospectives.
4. Expand Agile practices to other teams and refine based on feedback.

Celebrate each milestone to build momentum and keep the team motivated.

Prioritize Quick Wins

Nothing builds confidence like early success. Identify quick wins that demonstrate the value of Agile right away.

Examples of quick wins:

- Implement daily stand-ups to improve communication.

- Use kanban boards to visualize workflows and reduce bottlenecks.

- Involve stakeholders in sprint reviews to build trust and alignment.

Quick wins aren't about shortcuts—they're about proving that change works.

Aligning Stakeholders and Securing Leadership Buy-In

No transformation succeeds without the support of key stakeholders. They provide the resources, guidance, and advocacy needed to drive change. But getting their buy-in isn't always easy—it takes vision, strategy, and persistence.

Identify Your Stakeholders

Stakeholders aren't just leaders—they're anyone affected by the transformation. This includes:

- Executives and senior leadership.
- Team managers and department heads.
- Product owners and Scrum Masters.
- Customers and end-users.

Map out your stakeholders and understand their interests, concerns, and influence.

Speak to Their Needs

Different stakeholders care about different things. Tailor your message to address what matters most to them.

For example:

- **Executives:** Focus on business outcomes like faster delivery, improved customer satisfaction, and reduced costs.
- **Team Managers:** Highlight how Agile empowers their teams and reduces burnout.
- **Developers:** Emphasize how Agile eliminates unnecessary bureaucracy and fosters

creativity.

Address Resistance

Resistance is natural—it's a sign that people care about the change. Instead of dismissing it, engage with it.

Strategies for overcoming resistance:

- **Listen actively:** Understand their concerns and acknowledge their feelings.

- **Provide evidence:** Share success stories, case studies, and metrics that demonstrate Agile's value.

- **Involve them:** People are more likely to support what they help create. Include resistant stakeholders in planning and decision-making.

Launching Your Agile Pilot

The best way to start an Agile transformation is to start small. A pilot project allows you to test new practices, learn from real-world challenges, and build a foundation for scaling.

Choose the Right Team

Your pilot team should be:

- **Cross-functional:** Include members from all disciplines needed to deliver value, such as developers, testers, designers, and product owners.

- **Open-minded:** Look for individuals who are excited about trying new approaches.

- **Representative:** Choose a team whose success will inspire confidence across the organization.

Define the Scope

Start with a project that is:

- **Manageable:** Avoid overly complex or high-stakes initiatives.

- **Valuable:** Choose something that delivers visible benefits to stakeholders and customers.

- **Time-Bound:** Aim for a short timeframe, such as 2–4 sprints, to demonstrate results quickly.

Measure and Learn

Agile is all about adaptation, and your pilot project is no exception. Track progress using metrics like:

- Velocity: How much work is the team completing each sprint?
- Cycle time: How long does it take to deliver a single item of value?
- Stakeholder satisfaction: Are stakeholders happy with the process and results?

Gather feedback from the team and stakeholders to identify what's working and what needs improvement.

Building Momentum for Full-Scale Transformation

Once your pilot project is a success, it's time to scale. But scaling isn't just about replicating practices—it's about embedding Agile principles into the DNA of your organization.

Expand Gradually

Roll out Agile practices to other teams in phases. Provide training, mentorship, and support to ensure a smooth transition.

Invest in Leadership Development

Agile leaders play a critical role in guiding and sustaining transformation. Equip them with the tools and knowledge they need to succeed.

Focus on:

- Servant leadership: Empowering teams rather than dictating solutions.
- Change management: Navigating resistance and fostering a growth mindset.
- Metrics and feedback: Using data to drive continuous improvement.

Celebrate Wins, Big and Small

Transformation is a journey, not a destination. Celebrate every achievement, no matter how small, to keep the team motivated and engaged.

The Beginning of Something Extraordinary

Starting your Agile journey isn't just about adopting a new way of working—it's about embracing a new way of thinking. It's about creating an organization that's not only efficient and innovative but also resilient and empowering.

The road ahead won't always be easy, but it will always be worth it. With a clear vision, a strategic plan, and the commitment to continuous improvement, you have everything you need to succeed.

In the next chapter, we'll explore how to take your transformation to the next level by scaling Agile across the organization. Get ready to amplify your impact and drive lasting change!

Chapter 9 - Scaling Agile Across the Organization

Scaling Agile is not just about expanding practices—it's about expanding mindsets, capabilities, and impact. It's about taking what works on a team level and amplifying it across an entire organization, enabling collaboration, alignment, and agility at scale. But scaling comes with challenges. Missteps can lead to diluted values, increased complexity, and diminished returns.

In this chapter, we'll uncover the strategies, frameworks, and principles that enable successful scaling. From implementing frameworks like SAFe

(Scaled Agile Framework) to overcoming resistance, we'll give you the tools to create a culture of agility that drives results and sustains momentum.

Why Scale Agile?

Before diving into the "how," let's talk about the "why." Scaling Agile is about unleashing the power of alignment and collaboration across multiple teams, departments, or even geographies.

Unlocking Synergies Across Teams

When teams operate in silos, they miss opportunities for synergy. Scaling Agile creates connections, allowing teams to align on shared goals, coordinate dependencies, and deliver value as a unified force.

Responding to Complexity

As organizations grow, so does complexity. Scaling Agile provides the frameworks and structures needed to manage this complexity without losing the flexibility and speed that make Agile so powerful.

Accelerating Value Delivery

At its core, Agile is about delivering value faster. By scaling practices, you increase the capacity to deliver impactful results, driving competitive advantage and customer satisfaction.

Exploring Scaled Agile Frameworks

The beauty of Agile is its adaptability—but scaling requires structure. Frameworks like SAFe, LeSS (Large-Scale Scrum), and Scrum@Scale offer proven approaches for scaling Agile effectively.

Scaled Agile Framework (SAFe)

What is SAFe?
SAFe is a comprehensive framework designed to scale Agile practices across large organizations. It combines Agile principles with Lean thinking to deliver alignment, collaboration, and value at scale.

Core Components of SAFe:

- **Agile Release Train (ART):** A team of teams aligned around a shared mission, delivering value in synchronized increments.

- **Program Increment (PI) Planning:** A cadence-based planning event where teams align on objectives for the next iteration.

- **Lean Portfolio Management:** Aligning strategy and execution by connecting high-level business objectives to team-level work.

Pros of SAFe:

- Provides clear roles and processes for large organizations.

- Aligns strategic goals with team-level execution.

- Offers robust training and resources.

Cons of SAFe:

- Can feel rigid or overly complex for smaller organizations.

- Requires significant investment in training and adoption.

Large-Scale Scrum (LeSS)

What is LeSS? LeSS extends Scrum principles to multiple teams working on a single product. It emphasizes simplicity, minimizing roles and artifacts to maintain focus on delivering value.

Core Components of LeSS:

- **Single Product Backlog:** All teams share one backlog to prioritize work collectively.

- **Overall Retrospective:** Teams hold a joint retrospective to identify cross-team improvements.

- **Shared Sprint Review:** Teams come together to demonstrate progress and gather feedback.

Pros of LeSS:

- Retains the simplicity and flexibility of Scrum.
- Encourages strong collaboration and shared ownership.
- Ideal for organizations with a limited number of teams.

Cons of LeSS:

- May struggle with complexity in larger organizations.
- Requires a high level of coordination and trust among teams.

Scrum@Scale

What is Scrum@Scale? Developed by Scrum co-creator Jeff Sutherland, Scrum@Scale is a lightweight framework designed to scale Scrum by creating a fractal network of teams.

Core Components of Scrum@Scale:

- **Scrum of Scrums:** A coordination meeting where representatives from each team address cross-team dependencies.

- **Executive Action Team (EAT):** A leadership team responsible for removing organizational impediments and driving change.

- **Scaled Agile Metrics:** Metrics that track progress and alignment across all levels of the organization.

Pros of Scrum@Scale:

- Flexible and adaptable to different organizational structures.

- Retains Scrum's simplicity and lightweight nature.

- Focuses on scalability through decentralization.

Cons of Scrum@Scale:

- Requires strong facilitation and discipline to

maintain alignment.

- Limited prescriptive guidance may challenge teams new to scaling.

Overcoming Resistance to Scaling

Scaling Agile means change—and change often brings resistance. Whether it's fear of losing control, skepticism about Agile's effectiveness, or concerns about complexity, addressing resistance is critical to success.

Understanding the Roots of Resistance

Resistance usually stems from:

- **Fear of the Unknown:** People may resist because they don't understand what scaling will mean for them.

- **Past Failures:** If previous initiatives fell short, skepticism can take root.

- **Perceived Threats:** Managers may fear losing authority, while teams may worry about increased workload.

Strategies to Overcome Resistance

- **Educate and Empower:** Provide training, workshops, and resources to demystify scaling and build confidence.

- **Involve Stakeholders Early:** Include skeptics in planning and decision-making to address their concerns and gain their support.

- **Communicate the Why:** Clearly articulate the benefits of scaling, tying them to organizational goals and individual success.

- **Start Small:** Use pilot projects to demonstrate success and build momentum.

Strategies for Long-Term Agile Sustainability

Scaling isn't just about getting big—it's about staying Agile as you grow. Long-term sustainability requires intentional practices, continuous improvement, and a commitment to Agile values.

Fostering a Culture of Continuous Improvement

Encourage teams to:

- **Conduct Regular Retrospectives:** Reflect on what's working and what's not, making adjustments as needed.

- **Experiment and Innovate:** Give teams the freedom to test new ideas and processes.

- **Celebrate Learning:** Highlight lessons learned, not just successes, to reinforce the value of growth.

Investing in Agile Leadership

Agile leaders are the cornerstone of sustainability. They must:

- **Model Agile Values:** Demonstrate trust, transparency, and collaboration.

- **Coach Teams:** Support teams in overcoming challenges and reaching their full potential.

- **Drive Change:** Champion Agile practices and principles throughout the organization.

Measuring and Adapting

Track metrics that provide actionable insights into your scaling efforts:

- **Team Health Metrics:** Measure engagement, collaboration, and satisfaction.
- **Delivery Metrics:** Track cycle time, throughput, and predictability.
- **Business Impact Metrics:** Assess customer satisfaction, revenue growth, and market responsiveness.

Use these metrics to identify areas for improvement and guide decision-making.

Case Study: Scaling Success in Action

Let's look at a real-world example of scaling done right.

The Challenge: A global financial services company struggled with slow product delivery, misaligned teams, and a lack of customer focus.

The Approach:

- Adopted SAFe to align strategy with execution.

- Conducted PI Planning to synchronize teams and set shared goals.

- Trained leaders and teams in Agile principles and practices.

The Results:

- Reduced time-to-market by 40%.

- Improved collaboration across 25+ teams.

- Increased customer satisfaction through faster, more relevant product updates.

Key Takeaway: Scaling Agile isn't just about frameworks—it's about aligning people, processes, and goals to deliver extraordinary results.

Conclusion: Unleashing the Full Potential of Agile

Scaling Agile is about more than expanding practices—it's about creating an organization that's aligned, resilient, and ready to thrive in an ever-changing world. With the right frameworks, strategies, and mindset, you can overcome challenges, unlock synergies, and deliver value on a scale you never thought possible.

In the next chapter, we'll dive into real-world case studies and lessons learned, providing you with practical insights to guide your own Agile journey. Get ready to take your transformation to the next level!

Chapter 10 - Case Studies and Lessons Learned

Agile transformation is an exciting and challenging journey. It's not something that happens overnight, but rather, it's a series of steps, learnings, and adjustments that help organizations align, deliver value, and continuously improve. To truly master Agile excellence, we must look at real-world examples to understand how Agile principles can be applied in diverse industries, as well as how organizations overcome obstacles and build upon successes.

This chapter explores case studies from different industries, each with its own unique context, challenges, and solutions. We'll dive into lessons learned from both the successes and failures of Agile transformations, providing valuable insights for your own transformation journey. By understanding the pitfalls and triumphs of others, you can gain the clarity, wisdom, and confidence to accelerate your Agile adoption and transformation.

Case Study 1: Transforming a Global Financial Institution with SAFe

The Challenge: A global financial institution with thousands of employees across multiple regions had been facing slow product development cycles, poor communication across departments, and difficulty aligning strategic goals with day-to-day execution. Traditional project management approaches were no longer effective, and the company needed a way to scale Agile practices across its teams and departments while ensuring alignment with the organization's overarching goals.

The Approach: The organization decided to implement the Scaled Agile Framework (SAFe), a popular framework for scaling Agile across large enterprises. They began by training executives and managers to understand SAFe's core principles, including its focus on value streams, cross-functional collaboration, and alignment. The company rolled out SAFe incrementally, starting with a few key teams and expanding to include more departments.

The Execution:

- **ARTs (Agile Release Trains):** The organization formed Agile Release Trains (ARTs), which were teams of Agile teams that collaborated to deliver value in synchronized, timeboxed increments (Program Increments, or PIs). These ARTs included a mix of development teams, business stakeholders, and product owners working together to ensure alignment and focus on high-priority initiatives.

- **PI Planning:** Every 8-12 weeks, the company

held PI Planning sessions where all ART members came together to align on their goals, set deliverables, and identify potential blockers. These events encouraged transparent communication and fostered collaboration across previously siloed teams.

- **Lean Portfolio Management:** The company adopted Lean Portfolio Management practices to align strategic goals with execution. By using Kanban boards to track progress and manage flow, the organization could ensure that the work being done aligned with high-level business objectives and customer needs.

The Results:

- The financial institution saw significant improvements in speed and efficiency. Product development cycles shortened by 30%, and teams were able to respond more quickly to customer feedback.

- Cross-functional collaboration flourished,

leading to better decision-making and stronger alignment between development teams and business units.

- Despite initial resistance, the gradual, transparent rollout of SAFe helped build buy-in across the organization, and leadership's commitment to ongoing training and support was critical to long-term success.

Key Takeaways:

- Scaling Agile requires careful planning and alignment, particularly with larger organizations. The SAFe framework provided the structure needed for the financial institution to scale without compromising Agile's core values of collaboration and flexibility.

- Strong leadership and continuous communication were essential in overcoming initial resistance and building organizational commitment.

- In order to sustain Agile at scale, an organization must regularly assess its processes, invest in training, and refine its approach based on feedback from teams and stakeholders.

Case Study 2: Agile Transformation in a Software Startup

The Challenge: A software startup in the tech industry had experienced rapid growth, but their project delivery had become disorganized. With a small, cross-functional team, they had initially embraced Agile but struggled as their product and team grew. Lack of clarity around roles, fragmented communication, and inconsistent delivery timelines started to impact the company's growth and customer satisfaction.

The Approach: The leadership team recognized that they needed to formalize and scale their Agile practices to maintain their speed and quality of delivery. They decided to implement Scrum more rigorously while integrating elements of Lean to streamline processes and eliminate waste.

The Execution:

- **Scrum Implementation:** The team adopted Scrum ceremonies and artifacts, including sprint planning, daily standups, sprint reviews, and retrospectives. The roles of Scrum Master and Product Owner were clearly defined, and the teams took full ownership of their respective backlogs.

- **Kanban for Operational Efficiency:** To address bottlenecks in support and maintenance tasks, the team introduced Kanban boards to visualize workflows, prioritize work, and manage task flow. The goal was to reduce cycle times and ensure that customer support requests were handled quickly.

- **Cross-Functional Teams:** The company shifted from having separate development, design, and QA teams to creating fully cross-functional teams that worked on features end-to-end. This allowed for greater collaboration, quicker feedback loops, and faster delivery.

The Results:

- The company increased its ability to deliver features and improvements in shorter timeframes, reducing the cycle time by 40%.

- Team members reported higher satisfaction with their work, as they had more ownership and clarity around the goals and priorities.

- Communication between teams improved significantly, reducing the friction that had previously existed between development, design, and QA.

Key Takeaways:

- Even in smaller organizations, scaling Agile practices requires clarity around roles and workflows. By formalizing Scrum and introducing Lean practices, the company was able to better manage their growing responsibilities.

- Cross-functional teams are a key enabler of Agile success. The integration of design, development, and QA into single teams helped reduce silos and improved delivery timelines.

- Regular feedback loops (through sprint reviews and retrospectives) allowed the team to continuously improve their practices and deliver higher quality products to customers.

Case Study 3: Overcoming Resistance in a Healthcare Organization

The Challenge: A mid-sized healthcare organization was struggling to align its IT department with business objectives. They had implemented Agile at the team level but faced significant resistance from leadership and various functional departments, who viewed Agile as a threat to traditional hierarchical management structures. Additionally, regulatory compliance requirements added complexity to the process.

The Approach: Recognizing the need for organizational buy-in, the organization decided to engage leadership early in the process. They also focused on the tangible benefits that Agile could bring to customer satisfaction, regulatory compliance, and cost efficiency. The company began with a pilot project in a single department and worked to expand Agile practices from there.

The Execution:

- **Leadership Alignment:** Senior leadership was educated about the benefits of Agile, with a specific focus on how Agile could improve responsiveness to regulatory changes, patient care quality, and overall service delivery.

- **Cross-Functional Teams:** Agile teams were formed across functional areas, including IT, operations, and business teams, to ensure collaboration and cross-functional communication. These teams worked on creating a new patient management system with high visibility and priority.

- **Compliance and Risk Management:** The company collaborated with regulatory bodies to ensure that Agile processes were aligned with compliance standards. This included regular audits and checks to ensure that Agile workflows did not compromise patient data security or regulatory requirements.

The Results:

- After a successful pilot, Agile practices spread across the organization, improving both collaboration and delivery efficiency. The IT department's ability to respond to changing regulations and urgent business needs improved dramatically.

- The organization's ability to prioritize and respond to customer and regulatory needs became faster and more effective, leading to improved patient care and satisfaction.

- Leadership buy-in and alignment were critical for overcoming resistance and ensuring the sustainability of Agile practices.

Key Takeaways:

- Overcoming resistance to Agile requires targeted communication and education at all levels of the organization. By demonstrating how Agile could meet specific challenges (e.g., regulatory compliance), the company gained leadership support.

- Agile adoption is often a gradual process. Piloting Agile in one department or on a high-priority project can provide proof of concept before scaling.

- In regulated industries like healthcare, it is essential to adapt Agile practices to meet specific compliance and security requirements. Agile can coexist with stringent regulations if proper safeguards and processes are in place.

Conclusion: Learning from Real-World Transformations

Agile transformations are not one-size-fits-all. The diversity of industries, organizational structures, and team cultures means that each journey will be unique. However, there are common lessons that can guide your own transformation process.

- **Start with Leadership Buy-In:** Leadership support is critical. Without it, even the most well-intentioned Agile efforts can fail. Engage leaders early and make sure they understand the benefits and principles of Agile.

- **Adapt to Your Context:** Whether you're scaling Agile in a large organization or improving a small team's effectiveness, tailor your approach to your specific challenges. No single framework works for every organization.

- **Focus on Continuous Improvement:** Agile is all about evolution. Don't expect perfection from the start. Use feedback, retrospectives, and lessons learned to continuously refine your practices.

- **Communication is Key:** Whether you are scaling Agile or introducing it at the team level, clear, transparent, and frequent communication helps everyone stay aligned and focused on common goals.

By learning from these case studies, you can better understand the potential pitfalls and the success factors that contribute to Agile excellence. Embrace the journey of transformation with an open mind, and don't be afraid to adapt, experiment, and continuously improve. Your organization's Agile success is within reach.

Chapter 11 - Essential Agile Tools and Techniques

In the world of Agile, tools and techniques are not just conveniences—they are essential catalysts for continuous improvement, efficient communication, and high-performance execution. When implemented effectively, the right tools empower teams to unlock their full potential, overcome challenges, and ensure a smooth, productive flow of work. However, the tools are only as effective as the commitment and discipline with which they are applied.

This chapter will explore the core tools and techniques that are indispensable for successful

Agile project management. You'll gain insight into popular Agile tools like Jira, Trello, and Asana, and how they help teams visualize progress, manage workflows, and collaborate seamlessly. We'll dive deeper into the specific metrics that drive progress, like burndown charts, cumulative flow diagrams, and lead time metrics, and understand how to use them to measure success and identify areas for improvement.

Throughout this chapter, our goal is not only to introduce you to the essential tools and techniques but to empower you with the knowledge to leverage them strategically. By the end of this chapter, you'll be equipped with the tools to elevate your Agile practices, ensuring that your team and organization thrive in an Agile environment.

Understanding the Value of Agile Tools

Agile tools are more than just software applications; they are the cornerstone of high-performing teams. They are designed to simplify processes, enhance collaboration, increase transparency, and provide real-time feedback. When you use these tools correctly, they become enablers of Agile values like transparency, inspection, and adaptation.

Agile tools help:

- **Facilitate Collaboration**: Through centralized communication channels, teams can collaborate in real-time, breaking down silos and fostering transparency.

- **Visualize Workflows**: By visualizing workflows and progress, teams are empowered to spot bottlenecks, eliminate waste, and stay aligned with their goals.

- **Enable Continuous Feedback**: Agile tools create a feedback loop where teams can receive, analyze, and act on feedback faster, leading to continuous improvement.

- **Support Adaptability**: Agile tools offer the flexibility to manage changing priorities, so teams can remain adaptable in the face of evolving requirements.

As you progress in your Agile journey, your proficiency with these tools will greatly influence the speed and success of your transformation. So let's take a deeper dive into some of the most popular and effective tools in the Agile ecosystem.

Section 2: Popular Agile Tools for Project Management

Jira

Overview: Jira is one of the most widely-used Agile project management tools, particularly in software development environments. Developed by Atlassian, Jira is highly configurable and supports both Scrum and Kanban methodologies. It is known for its ability to scale from small teams to large enterprises, making it suitable for any organization on an Agile journey.

Key Features:

- **Customizable Workflows**: Jira's workflows are completely customizable, allowing teams to tailor their processes according to their specific needs.

- **Backlog Management**: Jira allows you to easily manage product backlogs, prioritize user stories, and track progress through sprints.

- **Sprint Planning and Tracking**: Teams can plan sprints, track progress using burndown charts, and easily adjust sprint goals based on team velocity and feedback.

- **Advanced Reporting**: Jira provides robust reporting tools like velocity charts, cumulative flow diagrams, and control charts, which help teams gain insights into their performance and identify areas for improvement.

When to Use Jira:

- For teams that need to manage complex backlogs and want to integrate with other tools in the Atlassian suite (such as Confluence and Bitbucket).

- For large teams or organizations looking to scale their Agile practices with a flexible tool.

- When you need detailed reporting and analytics to track team performance and sprint progress.

Trello

Overview: Trello is a simple, visual project management tool that uses boards, lists, and cards to manage work. It is particularly popular among small teams and those just starting on their Agile journey due to its intuitive design and ease of use.

Key Features:

- **Visual Task Management**: Trello's boards and cards allow teams to visually organize tasks, making it easy to understand the status of work at a glance.

- **Collaboration**: Teams can collaborate in

real-time, add comments, attachments, and due dates to cards, and link tasks to create dependencies.

- **Power-Ups**: Trello offers a wide variety of integrations with other tools (like Slack, Google Drive, and GitHub) to extend its capabilities.

When to Use Trello:

- For smaller teams or those with simpler workflows.

- When a visually appealing, easy-to-use tool is needed to get started quickly with Agile practices.

- For teams that prioritize simplicity over advanced features and detailed reporting.

Asana

Overview: Asana is another powerful project management tool that helps teams coordinate, track, and complete work. It is suitable for teams of all sizes and supports both Agile and traditional project management approaches.

Key Features:

- **Task Management**: Asana allows you to break down projects into tasks and sub-tasks, assign them to team members, and track progress.

- **Workflows**: You can create custom workflows and automate repetitive tasks, ensuring consistency and reducing manual effort.

- **Reporting and Dashboards**: Asana includes basic reporting tools and dashboards that allow you to visualize project status and team performance.

When to Use Asana:

- For teams that need a balance of simplicity and functionality, with an emphasis on task management and collaboration.

- When you want to track progress without getting bogged down in complex reporting or advanced configurations.

- For teams that want flexibility and integrations with other tools while still maintaining a simple, user-friendly interface.

Agile Techniques for Project Success

While tools are indispensable for Agile project management, it is the techniques that truly drive team success. In this section, we'll explore the essential Agile techniques that complement the tools you use.

Burndown Charts

What It Is: A burndown chart is a visual representation of the work remaining in a sprint or project. It is one of the most powerful tools for monitoring progress, and it provides an immediate snapshot of how much work remains compared to how much time is left.

How to Use It:

- Track the number of tasks or story points left to complete over time.

- Update the chart daily during the sprint to show the remaining work.

- Use the burndown chart to identify scope creep, potential delays, or areas where the team might be over- or under-performing.

Benefits:

- Provides transparency into the progress of a sprint or project.

- Helps identify potential blockers early.

- Motivates teams by showing how much work has been completed, fostering a sense of accomplishment.

Cumulative Flow Diagram (CFD)

What It Is: A cumulative flow diagram (CFD) is a tool used to track the flow of work items through various stages in a Kanban system. It visually displays the status of work in progress and highlights bottlenecks and areas that need attention.

How to Use It:

- Track work through columns such as "To Do," "In Progress," and "Done."

- Analyze the flow of work to identify delays or inefficiencies in the process.

- Use the diagram to optimize workflows and ensure that work is progressing smoothly from start to finish.

Benefits:

- Offers a clear, real-time view of work in progress.

- Helps detect bottlenecks or inefficiencies in the workflow.

- Provides data for process optimization and improvement.

Lead Time and Cycle Time

What They Are: Lead time refers to the total time from when a work item is requested to when it is completed, while cycle time focuses specifically on the time taken to complete a work item once it starts.

How to Use Them:

- Measure both lead time and cycle time to identify delays and improve the efficiency of your processes.

- Focus on reducing cycle time to deliver value faster and more consistently.

- Use these metrics to gauge the efficiency of your Agile practices and refine them over time.

Benefits:

- Help track the efficiency and effectiveness of your workflow.

- Support the continuous improvement mindset by identifying areas for process optimization.

- Provide data-driven insights that can help you make more informed decisions about how to improve team performance.

Choosing the Right Metrics to Measure Success

Effective metrics are critical in any Agile environment. They provide actionable insights into team performance, product quality, and overall project health. In this section, we will examine the key metrics that every Agile team should track.

Velocity

Velocity measures how much work a team completes during a sprint, typically measured in story points. It is an important metric for predicting how much work can be accomplished in future sprints.

How to Use It:

- Track the number of story points completed in each sprint.

- Use historical velocity data to predict how much work can be completed in future sprints.

- Ensure that the velocity is stable and avoid overloading teams.

Team Happiness

While it's important to measure the speed at which work is completed, measuring the well-being and engagement of your team is just as important. Team happiness surveys and regular check-ins allow you to assess the emotional and psychological state of your team.

How to Use It:

- Use regular surveys or feedback sessions to gauge the mood and satisfaction of your team.

- Ensure that teams are not burning out by tracking work-life balance and overall job satisfaction.

Conclusion

Mastering Agile tools and techniques is a journey, one that requires consistent effort, learning, and refinement. The tools you use should support your Agile principles, not dictate them. With the right tools in place, teams can work more efficiently, collaborate more effectively, and continuously improve. However, remember that the ultimate goal is not just the tools you use, but the impact they have on the team's performance and the organization's ability to deliver value.

By integrating Agile tools and techniques into your daily workflow, you create an environment where success is not a matter of chance but a matter of consistency and alignment with your Agile values. The true power of Agile comes not from the software or metrics themselves, but from how you use them to transform your team and organization. Stay committed, stay focused, and continue mastering the tools and techniques that drive Agile excellence!

Chapter 12 - Templates for Agile Teams

Agile methodologies are all about adaptability, efficiency, and continuous improvement. However, achieving these goals doesn't just happen by chance—it requires clear structures and systems that help teams stay organized, focused, and aligned. One of the most powerful tools in the Agile arsenal is the template. These simple yet effective tools act as blueprints for various processes and ceremonies within Agile teams, allowing them to follow a proven structure while still maintaining the flexibility to innovate.

In this chapter, we will explore a variety of Agile templates designed to facilitate common activities such as sprint planning, retrospectives, backlog management, and more. These templates will serve as both foundational tools and dynamic guides to ensure that your team remains on track, stays aligned with Agile principles, and achieves consistent, high-quality results.

Whether you are just starting out with Agile or you're looking to refine your practices, these templates will help streamline your workflow, reduce friction in your processes, and free up time for creativity and innovation.

The Importance of Templates in Agile Teams

Before diving into specific templates, it's important to understand why they play such a crucial role in Agile teams. Templates provide structure while allowing for flexibility—two key pillars of the Agile mindset. They offer a consistent framework for teams to follow, ensuring that nothing falls through the cracks.

But, just as importantly, templates are dynamic tools that can be adapted to suit the evolving needs of your team.

The right templates can:

- **Reduce Cognitive Load**: By providing a predefined structure, templates help team members focus on the task at hand without worrying about formatting or process details.

- **Increase Consistency**: Templates standardize processes, making it easier for teams to align on expectations, work methods, and deliverables.

- **Facilitate Communication**: When everyone is using the same templates, it becomes much easier to communicate, share information, and track progress.

- **Enhance Collaboration**: Templates can help break down complex activities (like retrospectives or sprint planning) into manageable, collaborative steps, making it easier for everyone to contribute and stay engaged.

Now, let's explore the specific templates that every Agile team should be using.

Sprint Planning Templates

Sprint planning is one of the most important events in the Agile process. It sets the tone for the entire sprint, aligning the team on the goals, tasks, and deliverables for the upcoming cycle. A well-structured sprint planning meeting ensures that the team starts the sprint with clarity and focus.

Sprint Planning Template:

1. **Sprint Goal**: Define the primary objective for the sprint. What is the team trying to achieve by the end of the sprint?

2. **Backlog Items**: Review and prioritize the items from the product backlog. This could include user stories, technical tasks, or bug fixes.

3. **Task Breakdown**: For each selected backlog item, break it down into smaller, actionable tasks. These tasks should be small enough to be completed within the sprint timeframe.

4. **Estimation**: Estimate the effort required for each task, usually in story points or hours. This helps determine the team's capacity for the sprint.

5. **Sprint Commitment**: Agree on which backlog items the team will commit to completing by the end of the sprint.

6. **Dependencies and Risks**: Identify any dependencies, roadblocks, or risks that might affect the sprint's progress.

By using a template like this, you ensure that your sprint planning meetings are focused, efficient, and aligned with the team's goals.

Retrospective Templates

The retrospective is a powerful tool for continuous improvement. It provides a dedicated time for the team to reflect on the previous sprint, discuss what went well, identify areas for improvement, and agree on concrete actions to make the next sprint more effective.

Retrospective Template:

1. **Start, Stop, Continue**:
    - **Start**: What new practices or behaviors should the team start implementing?
    - **Stop**: What ineffective practices or behaviors should the team stop doing?
    - **Continue**: What's working well and should continue to be a part of the team's process?
2. **What Went Well?**: Identify the positive aspects of the sprint. What were the successes? What did the team do right?
3. **What Could Have Gone Better?**: Discuss the challenges and obstacles faced during the sprint. What can be improved in the future?

4. **Actionable Items**: Create concrete, actionable items for improvement. These should be specific and measurable actions that can be tested in the next sprint.

5. **Team Appreciation**: End on a positive note by expressing gratitude and appreciation for each other's contributions.

This template helps guide the retrospective conversation, ensuring that it's constructive and focused on continuous improvement.

Backlog Prioritization Templates

An essential part of any Agile framework is the management of the product backlog. The backlog is a dynamic list of tasks, user stories, and features that need to be completed. Prioritizing the backlog ensures that the team is always working on the most valuable items, allowing for faster delivery of customer value.

Backlog Prioritization Template:

1. **Backlog Item Name**: A brief description of the task or feature.

2. **Business Value**: Rate the importance or business value of the item (e.g., low, medium, high).

3. **Effort Estimation**: Estimate the effort required to complete the item (e.g., small, medium, large).

4. **Priority**: Rank the item's priority relative to other items in the backlog. High-priority items should be completed first.

5. **Dependencies**: List any dependencies or requirements that must be completed before starting this item.

6. **Acceptance Criteria**: Define clear criteria for what constitutes the completion of this item.

This template helps ensure that your backlog is always prioritized effectively, allowing the team to focus on the most important tasks first and deliver maximum value.

Workflow Board Templates

A visual representation of the workflow is essential for tracking progress, identifying bottlenecks, and ensuring that tasks are moving smoothly through the process. A well-organized workflow board, whether in a Kanban system or Scrum framework, helps teams manage their work efficiently.

Kanban Workflow Board Template:

1. **To Do**: The backlog items that need to be worked on.

2. **In Progress**: Items that are currently being worked on.

3. **Blocked**: Items that are facing issues or roadblocks and need attention.

4. **Ready for Review**: Items that are complete and need to be reviewed before moving to completion.

5. **Done**: Completed items that have passed the review and are ready for deployment or release.

This simple yet powerful board helps teams visualize their work, identify potential delays, and maintain a steady flow of tasks.

Daily Stand-up Templates

The daily stand-up meeting is a critical Agile ceremony. It's a quick, focused meeting that ensures everyone on the team is aligned on the day's goals and any potential issues are flagged early. A template helps ensure that the stand-up is focused and time-efficient.

Daily Stand-up Template:

1. **What did I do yesterday?**: Each team member briefly shares what they accomplished in the previous day.

2. **What will I do today?**: Each team member outlines what they plan to accomplish today.

3. **Any blockers or challenges?**: Team members flag any obstacles that are preventing them from making progress.

This template keeps the stand-up focused on key information, reducing the risk of the meeting becoming a lengthy or unfocused discussion.

Conclusion

Templates are more than just "nice-to-haves"—they are integral to the success of Agile teams. They provide structure, help teams stay organized, and ensure that key processes are followed. Whether you are preparing for a sprint planning session, conducting a retrospective, or prioritizing your backlog, these templates will help streamline your workflow, improve collaboration, and ultimately drive success.

As you begin to incorporate these templates into your Agile practices, remember that they are not rigid frameworks—they are flexible tools that can be adapted to fit the needs of your team. Don't be afraid to adjust them as you see fit, based on your team's size, maturity, and specific goals. By making these templates a part of your Agile routine, you are setting your team up for consistent success, continuous improvement, and ultimately, Agile excellence.

By using the right templates, you are empowering your team to focus on what truly matters—delivering high-quality, valuable products, improving your processes, and growing together. So, take these templates, integrate them into your Agile practices, and watch your team evolve into a well-oiled, high-performing machine. The tools are there, the structure is in place—now it's time to unlock your team's full potential.

Chapter 13 - Resources for Continuous Learning

As you embark on the journey of mastering Agile excellence, one thing becomes abundantly clear: continuous learning is the key to success. The Agile mindset is not just about following processes or completing projects; it is about embracing change, constantly improving, and growing both as individuals and as a team. Just as the world of business and technology is always evolving, so too must your skills, knowledge, and approaches to Agile practices.

In this final chapter, we will explore the resources that can empower you to deepen your Agile expertise, whether you are just beginning your journey or you are already an experienced practitioner seeking to take your abilities to the next level. We'll cover recommended books, online courses, certifications, and strategies for building a personal development plan for Agile mastery.

As with any professional endeavor, your growth in Agile will require commitment, persistence, and a proactive approach. The more you immerse yourself in learning, the more equipped you will be to handle the complexities and challenges of Agile transformations, leadership, and team dynamics.

Let's dive in.

Recommended Books for Agile Mastery

Books are an incredible resource for deepening your understanding of Agile. They provide foundational knowledge, expert insights, and practical frameworks that can be applied in real-world scenarios. Below is a list of essential books that will help you on your path to mastering Agile principles and practices.

1. **"The Lean Startup" by Eric Ries** This book introduces the Lean methodology, which shares many principles with Agile, such as customer-driven development, iterative processes, and continuous feedback. Whether you're a product owner, manager, or entrepreneur, "The Lean Startup" provides valuable lessons on how to approach projects with a mindset of testing, learning, and adapting.

2. **"Scrum: The Art of Doing Twice the Work in Half the Time" by Jeff Sutherland** Written by one of the creators of Scrum, this book is a must-read for anyone adopting Scrum. It offers practical advice, real-world examples, and insights into how Scrum can help you optimize your team's performance and deliver more value in less time.

3. **"Kanban: Successful Evolutionary Change**

for Your Technology Business" by David J. Anderson** If you're interested in the Kanban framework, this is the definitive guide. Anderson explains how to implement Kanban, manage workflow, and improve delivery times. It's a great resource for anyone looking to introduce Kanban into their organization or fine-tune their existing Kanban processes.

4. **"The Phoenix Project: A Novel About IT, DevOps, and Helping Your Business Win" by Gene Kim, Kevin Behr, and George Spafford** While not exclusively focused on Agile, this novel is essential for understanding the broader context of Agile, DevOps, and IT transformation. Written as a narrative, it follows the story of an IT manager tasked with saving a troubled project, illustrating many principles of Agile, Lean, and DevOps in action.

5. **"The Agile Samurai: How Agile Masters Deliver Great Software" by Jonathan

Rasmusson This book is an accessible yet comprehensive guide to Agile software development. It covers key Agile practices, the roles involved in Agile teams, and how to execute successful sprints. It's especially valuable for those looking for a hands-on, practical approach to Agile.

6. **"Drive: The Surprising Truth About What Motivates Us" by Daniel H. Pink** While not an Agile-specific book, "Drive" is an essential read for anyone leading an Agile team. It explores the psychology of motivation, providing valuable insights into how you can create a work environment that encourages innovation, autonomy, and mastery—core tenets of the Agile mindset.

7. **"The Lean Enterprise: How High Performance Organizations Innovate at Scale" by Jez Humble, Joanne Molesky, and Barry O'Reilly** This book focuses on applying Lean principles to large organizations, making it a great resource for those scaling

Agile across enterprises. It provides insights into how to build a culture of continuous innovation, even in complex, large-scale environments.

Online Courses and Certifications

While books are a fantastic resource, hands-on experience is equally important. Online courses offer you the opportunity to dive deeper into Agile frameworks and acquire certifications that validate your knowledge and skills. Here are some of the best online courses and certifications available:

1. **Certified ScrumMaster (CSM) by Scrum Alliance** The CSM certification is one of the most popular and widely recognized certifications for Scrum practitioners. The course is typically a two-day workshop led by a certified Scrum trainer, where you will learn the fundamentals of Scrum, the roles within Scrum, and how to facilitate Scrum

ceremonies. It's an excellent choice for anyone looking to become a Scrum Master or deepen their understanding of Scrum.

2. **Certified Scrum Product Owner (CSPO) by Scrum Alliance** If you're a product owner or aspire to be one, the CSPO certification is essential. The course covers the responsibilities of a product owner, including backlog management, stakeholder communication, and creating a product vision. The certification is perfect for individuals looking to work closely with Scrum teams and drive product success.

3. **Kanban System Design by Kanban University** This is the foundational certification course for anyone wanting to learn Kanban in depth. The course covers the basics of Kanban, including its principles, the flow of work, and how to implement Kanban in real-world scenarios. It's a great option for anyone transitioning from Scrum to Kanban or looking to deepen their Kanban

knowledge.

4. **Agile Project Management by PMI** The Project Management Institute (PMI) offers a comprehensive course on Agile project management, which is ideal for individuals who want to combine traditional project management with Agile practices. This course covers Agile methodologies, including Scrum, Kanban, and Lean, and how to manage projects using Agile principles.

5. **Lean Six Sigma Certification** Lean Six Sigma is a methodology focused on reducing waste and improving process efficiency. It integrates well with Agile principles, particularly in terms of delivering value and continuous improvement. Lean Six Sigma certifications are offered at various levels (Green Belt, Black Belt, etc.) and can be particularly useful if you're looking to blend Lean and Agile practices within your organization.

6. **Coursera and edX Agile Courses** Online

platforms like Coursera and edX offer numerous Agile-related courses from universities such as the University of Virginia, University of California, and others. These courses range from introductory to advanced levels and can help you build foundational knowledge or enhance your existing skills.

Building a Personal Development Plan for Agile Mastery

While taking courses and reading books is an excellent way to grow your knowledge, mastering Agile is an ongoing process of self-development. To truly become an Agile expert, you need to develop a personal learning plan that aligns with your career goals and the needs of your organization.

Here's how you can build your personal development plan for Agile mastery:

1. **Assess Your Current Skill Level** Before diving

into new resources, take a moment to reflect on where you are now. Assess your strengths and areas for improvement within Agile practices. Are you comfortable with Scrum, or do you need more experience in Kanban? Do you have a solid understanding of Agile leadership, or are you still learning how to guide teams?

2. **Set Clear Learning Goals** Once you've assessed your current skill level, set specific, measurable, achievable, relevant, and time-bound (SMART) goals for your Agile learning journey. For example, "In the next six months, I will complete the Scrum Master certification and apply Scrum in my team's workflow." Break down larger goals into smaller steps, and track your progress over time.

3. **Immerse Yourself in the Agile Community** The Agile community is vast and filled with experts, practitioners, and enthusiasts eager to share their knowledge. Participate in

forums, attend conferences, and join local or virtual Agile meetups. Learning from others can expand your perspective and expose you to different approaches to Agile.

4. **Apply Agile Practices** It's not enough to just read books and take courses—you need to apply what you learn in real-world situations. Look for opportunities within your current role or organization to apply Agile principles. Whether it's leading a sprint or facilitating a retrospective, hands-on experience is essential for deepening your understanding and building your confidence.

5. **Seek Feedback and Mentorship** Learning is accelerated when you have a mentor or feedback from experienced practitioners. Find someone who can guide you through the challenges of Agile adoption, provide insights, and help you refine your approach. Regular feedback from peers and leaders will also help you grow and refine your skills.

6. **Stay Updated with Industry Trends** Agile is

an evolving field, with new frameworks, tools, and best practices emerging all the time. Stay current with the latest developments by subscribing to industry blogs, following Agile thought leaders on social media, and reading research papers and case studies.

7. **Embrace Continuous Improvement** One of the key tenets of Agile is continuous improvement—and that applies to your personal development as well. Regularly revisit your goals, adjust your learning plan, and stay open to new approaches. The journey of mastering Agile is ongoing, so adopt a mindset of lifelong learning and growth.

Conclusion

Mastering Agile excellence is not a destination; it is a journey—one that requires dedication, commitment, and a proactive approach to learning. By leveraging the resources outlined in this chapter—books, courses, certifications, and a personal development plan—you can accelerate your growth and become a true expert in Agile methodologies.

Remember, Agile is not just a set of practices; it's a mindset, a way of approaching challenges with creativity, flexibility, and a relentless focus on improvement. As you continue to learn and apply Agile principles, you will not only improve the way your teams work but also transform the way your organization delivers value to its customers.

So, keep learning, keep growing, and keep embracing the principles of Agile excellence. Your journey to mastering Agile is just beginning, and the possibilities are limitless.

platforms like Coursera and edX offer numerous Agile-related courses from universities such as the University of Virginia, University of California, and others. These courses range from introductory to advanced levels and can help you build foundational knowledge or enhance your existing skills.

Building a Personal Development Plan for Agile Mastery

While taking courses and reading books is an excellent way to grow your knowledge, mastering Agile is an ongoing process of self-development. To truly become an Agile expert, you need to develop a personal learning plan that aligns with your career goals and the needs of your organization.

Here's how you can build your personal development plan for Agile mastery:

1. **Assess Your Current Skill Level** Before diving

into new resources, take a moment to reflect on where you are now. Assess your strengths and areas for improvement within Agile practices. Are you comfortable with Scrum, or do you need more experience in Kanban? Do you have a solid understanding of Agile leadership, or are you still learning how to guide teams?

2. **Set Clear Learning Goals** Once you've assessed your current skill level, set specific, measurable, achievable, relevant, and time-bound (SMART) goals for your Agile learning journey. For example, "In the next six months, I will complete the Scrum Master certification and apply Scrum in my team's workflow." Break down larger goals into smaller steps, and track your progress over time.

3. **Immerse Yourself in the Agile Community** The Agile community is vast and filled with experts, practitioners, and enthusiasts eager to share their knowledge. Participate in

www.ingramcontent.com/pod-product-compliance
Lightning Source LLC
Chambersburg PA
CBHW071539220526
45469CB00003B/853